Modern C++ Coding Standards

A Zero-Fluff Guide to Modern C++ Best Practices,
Templates, and Compile-Time Programming.

by Marcus Tomlinson

Dedication

To my beautiful daughter Isla.

Contents

About The Author

Marcus Tomlinson is a qualified BSc Software Engineer and Author with well over a decade's experience in both closed- and open-source, cross-platform software development.

Immediately following his university career, Marcus landed his first job at Africa's leading manufacturer of electronic security products: IDS, where at the age of 21, he co-created a modular test jig system to help the company keep up with its rapidly growing product demand (A system that is still in effect today).

At 25, he went on to land his first senior role at the world's largest supplier of military and mining simulators: ThoroughTec, making him the youngest employee to hold the position. During his time there, Marcus completely overhauled the company's internal audio engine, as well as created a data-flow framework to modularise and simulate complex vehicle control systems.

In late 2013, Marcus landed a job at the open-source software giant: Canonical, designing and developing the Ubuntu Unity Shell. From 2013 to 2016, he rose up the ranks from Engineer to Technical Lead on the Ubuntu Personal team, and presented at a number of open-source developer summits.

Marcus has since served as Committee Chairman at The Computer Science Association of South Africa, developed software for the UK Government, worked with the Flutter team at Google, and written multiple critically acclaimed publications on programming, career development, and engineering management.

Introduction

Modern C++ Resource Management

Before getting into any coding standards, it's important that we first acknowledge what is arguably the most significant improvement C++ has seen since pre-2011: the codification of RAII.

Take smart pointers for example: In the classic C++ world, "cleaning up" a pointer meant determining exactly when its resource was no longer needed, then explicitly deallocating it at that point. In modern C++, we no longer need (or want) to determine upfront when a pointer is no longer needed. We simply define how it should be cleaned up, then rely on the language to determine when that is done. This idiom is of course RAII (resource acquisition is initialization) and has existed in C++ since day one, what C++11 did however, was codify it (in this case, with smart pointers) to make it easier for programmers to leverage.

RAII is not just a memory management tool though, it's useful in virtually any scoped set-up and tear-down scenario. A good example of this is the "lock guard". A lock guard is an object that manages a mutex by keeping it locked for as long as the guard is in scope. When the guard falls out of scope, it unlocks the mutex. A particular advantage to this (as opposed to manual locking and unlocking) is the guarantee that the mutex will always be unlocked upon leaving the scope, even if an exception is thrown mid-way.

Features such as these have tremendously improved the way resource management is handled in C++, and should be both appreciated and practiced in any modern C++ application today.

The Structure of This Book

This book is split into three parts:

Part One: Modern C++ Coding Standards

2021 (when I started this book) marked 10 years since the release of C++11, and the evolution from "classical" to "modern" C++. I thought it a good time to share some of the coding standards I've adopted over the past decade. No, not the kind that sweats the small stuff like formatting, naming conventions, or comment style - when it comes to these things, I say just pick a direction upfront, and keep consistent. What I want to share are a handful of simple guidelines and best practices I've personally utilized in producing (if I can say so myself) some solid C++ projects these last few years.

In this part we examine some modern C++ best practices by means of five minimal example listings: two C++ class headers, their two associated source files, and one main.cpp file.

Part Two: Language-Agnostic Best Practices

While preparing content for part one, a bunch of language-agnostic practices came to mind that were not specific to C++.

The advice in this part should be applicable to any programming language, although, considering how many variations in semantics and paradigms there are, it's almost certain to enter into a grey area here and there. At the very least, if a suggestion I make can't be applied directly to some other language, it should be applicable to some degree.

Part Three: Templates & Compile-Time Programming

Parts one and two (like many other books of this nature) cover only the "traditional" runtime programming side of C++. While templates and other forms of compile-time programming have been around for many years, modern C++ has seen vast improvements to this side of the language.

Considering the general lack of real understanding about (and thus, usage of) templates and compile-time programming amongst many C++ developers today, I thought it better to structure this part as more of an introduction to the current state of affairs, and where possible, throw in a few guidelines here and there.

PART ONE

MODERN C++ CODING STANDARDS

CHAPTER ONE

Class Headers

Base.h

```
101 | #pragma once
102 |
103 | #include <string>
104 | #include <vector>
105 |
106 | namespace CppCodingStandards
107 | {
108 |
109 | class Base
110 | {
111 | public:
112 |   Base();
113 |   virtual ~Base();
114 |
115 |   Base( const Base& ) = delete;
116 |   Base& operator=( const Base& ) = delete;
117 |
118 |   virtual void Print( const
          std::vector<std::string>& msg ) const = 0;
119 | };
120 |
121 | }  // namespace CppCodingStandards
```

Derived.h

```
201 | #pragma once
202 |
203 | #include <Base.h>
204 |
205 | #include <memory>
206 |
207 | namespace CppCodingStandards
208 | {
210 | namespace Private
211 | {
212 | class DerivedImpl;
213 | }
214 |
215 | class Derived final : public Base
216 | {
217 | public:
218 |   enum class State
219 |   {
220 |     Enabled,
221 |     Disabled
222 |   };
223 |
224 |   explicit Derived( State state );
225 |   ~Derived();
226 |
227 |   Derived( const Derived& ) = delete;
228 |   Derived& operator=( const Derived& ) = delete;
229 |
230 |   void Print( const std::vector<std::string>&
            msg ) const override;
231 |
232 |   float SlowlyGetPi( int newWaitTime = -1 );
233 |
234 | private:
235 |   std::unique_ptr<Private::DerivedImpl> p;
236 | };
237 |
238 | }  // namespace CppCodingStandards
```

From the Top...

- Use #pragma once at the top of every header to ensure that the file is included only once per compilation. **(101, 201)**

- #include as little as possible in your headers. Prefer to forward declare. This not only improves compilation time, but honours the greater rule of: "only make public what should be public". **(203, 212)**

- Avoid global using's in a header (That goes for namespaces and for aliases). They will pollute the global namespace of all source files that include it.

Inheritance

- Avoid declaring methods virtual until you have a valid and compelling reason for it. An abstract base class is a good example of such. **(118)**

- Explicitly declare overriding functions override. It's often better to be explicit than implicit. **(230)**

- Child classes should inherit to be re-usable, not to re-use. If a class is not designed to be a parent, use final to block any further inheritance. **(215)**

- Don't use private or protected inheritance. Keep it simple, always public inherit, and use multiple inheritance judiciously. **(215)**

Construction / Destruction

- Compilers implicitly generate a default constructor, destructor, copy constructor, and copy operator. Rather be explicit with them upfront, than face any nasty surprises later. **(112-116, 224-228)**

- Compilers will only implicitly generate a default move constructor and operator if there are no explicit destructors, copy constructors, or copy operators. However, if a class contains any non-movable, non-static members, the move operator will be deleted.

- **Always make base class destructors public and virtual.** This avoids memory leaking when an instance of a derived class is deleted through a pointer to its base. **(113)**

- Class copying is tricky. As a rule-of-thumb, disable copy operators upfront with =delete, and re-enable them only if your class absolutely requires it later. **(115-116, 227-228)**

- Consider using the explicit keyword before the declaration of any constructor with a single argument. This avoids classes being constructed implicitly by value. **(224)**

- Never throw an exception from the destructor, and never call a virtual method from either the constructor or the destructor.

Public Class Structure

- All classes, whether public or private, should belong to a namespace. Explicitly draw project boundary lines. **(106, 207, 210)**

- Always declare class members private. Again: "only make public what should be public". **(234-235)**

- Use the "pImpl" idiom to keep implementation details (private methods and members) out of public headers. **(235)**

- Try to avoid using friend classes. They tend to indicate poor design, and can allow users to gain access to all protected and private members of your API.

Method Declarations

- Prefer enum class over enum. They're type safe, and can be forward-declared unlike regular enums. **(218)**

- Prefer enums to booleans in method signatures to improve code readability, usability and safety. **(224)**

- Ensure that your API is const correct. That goes for both method const-ness as well as parameter const-ness. **(118, 230)**

- Prefer passing a non-trivial, non-mutable object as a const reference over passing it by value. This avoids the unnecessary overhead of copying the object into the method. **(118, 230)**

- Avoid using inline methods until you have proven that your code has a significant performance issue, and have confirmed that inlining fixes it.

CHAPTER TWO

Class Sources

Base.cpp

```
301 | #include <Base.h>
302 |
303 | using namespace CppCodingStandards;
304 |
305 | Base::Base() = default;
306 | Base::~Base() = default;
```

Derived.cpp

```
401 | #include <Derived.h>
402 |
403 | #include <iostream>
404 | #include <mutex>
405 | #include <thread>
406 |
407 | using namespace CppCodingStandards;
408 |
409 | static const float PI = 3.14159265359f;
410 |
```

```
411 |  namespace CppCodingStandards::Private
412 |  {
413 |
414 |  class DerivedImpl
415 |  {
416 |  public:
417 |    explicit DerivedImpl( Derived::State state )
418 |      : state( state )
419 |    {
420 |    }
421 |
422 |    int waitTime = 1;
423 |    const Derived::State state;
424 |    std::mutex mutex;
425 |  };
426 |
427 |  }  // namespace CppCodingStandards::Private
428 |
429 |  Derived::Derived( State state )
430 |    : p( std::make_unique<Private::DerivedImpl>
            ( state ) )
431 |  {
432 |  }
433 |
434 |  Derived::~Derived() = default;
435 |
436 |  void Derived::Print( const
          std::vector<std::string>& msg ) const
437 |  {
438 |    if ( p->state == State::Disabled )
439 |    {
440 |      return;
441 |    }
442 |
443 |    for ( const auto& string : msg )
444 |    {
445 |      std::cout << string << std::endl;
446 |    }
447 |  }
448 |
```

```
449 | float Derived::SlowlyGetPi( int newWaitTime )
450 | {
451 |   std::lock_guard<std::mutex> lock( p->mutex );
452 |
453 |   if ( newWaitTime >= 0 )
454 |   {
455 |     p->waitTime = newWaitTime;
456 |   }
457 |
458 |   std::this_thread::sleep_for
          ( std::chrono::seconds( p->waitTime ) );
459 |
460 |   return PI;
461 | }
```

From the Top...

- To guarantee completeness of your own headers, the order of items at the top of a source file should go:
  - Your header #includes **(401)**
  - Third-party header #includes
  - Standard header #includes **(403-405)**
  - usings **(407)**
  - static consts **(409)**

- Always prefer to #include using angle brackets over quotation marks. Project include paths should be configured in project config. **(401-405)**

- Don't pull in third-party dependencies unnecessarily. If there's already a standard feature available for what you need, use it. **(405, 458)**

- Use static consts instead of #define macros. A #define is just dumb text-replacement, it does not define an actual object. **(409)**

Private Class Structure

- All methods and members of a private pImpl class can be declared public as they are already only accessible to the owning class. **(416)**

- In-class initialize where possible. It is generally a good idea to initialize a variable on the same line that it is declared. **(422)**

- Where in-class initialization is not possible, prefer constructor initialization to assignment. This avoids unnecessary run-time overhead. **(418, 430)**

Method Definition / Implementation

- Always define methods in a .cpp file, even if they are just =default. This will keep the option of making changes to them open, without having to break the public interface. **(305-306)**

- Prefer lock guards and / or std::atomic variables over manual mutex locking and unlocking. **(424, 451)**

- The container rule-of-thumb: When in doubt use std::vector. Otherwise, choose a content-appropriate alternative (such as std::map or std::string). **(436)**

- Adopt a const iterator model for traversing linear data structures. Range-for loops have simpler syntax, and are generally faster and safer than indexed for loops. **(443)**

CHAPTER THREE

Application Sources

main.cpp

```
501 | #include <Derived.h>
502 |
503 | #include <future>
504 | #include <iostream>
505 |
506 | using namespace CppCodingStandards;
507 |
508 | template <typename T>
509 | using SPtr = std::shared_ptr<T>;
510 |
511 | int main()
512 | {
513 |   SPtr<Base> base = std::make_shared
          <Derived>( Derived::State::Enabled );
514 |
515 |   auto piFunction = [base]()
516 |   {
517 |     auto derived = std::dynamic_pointer_cast
          <Derived>( base );
518 |
519 |     if ( derived != nullptr )
520 |     {
521 |       return derived->SlowlyGetPi();
522 |     }
523 |
524 |     return 0.0f;
525 |   };
526 |
```

```
527 |     auto pi = std::async
              ( std::launch::async, piFunction );
528 |
529 |     base->Print( { "1", "two", "11", "0x4" } );
530 |
531 |     std::cout << "Pi: " << pi.get();
532 |
533 |     return 0;
534 | }
```

More on Implementation

- Prefer aliases over typedefs, and again, do not use #define macros. Alias syntax is simpler than typedef, especially with templated types. **(509, 513)**

- auto and decltype are great tools to have, but like templates, be aware of how they infer their types - e.g. decltype(auto) retains references and cv-qualifiers, while auto does not. **(443, 515, 517, 527)**

- In 99% of cases auto just works, but sometimes it makes more sense to be explicit. **(513)**

- Use std::function in place of old-style function pointers, and prefer lambdas over std::bind where anonymous functions are required. **(515, 527)**

- Prefer nullptr to NULL. The former is an actual null object, the latter is nothing more than a #define for the literal 0. **(519)**

- Prefer task-based programming to thread-based where possible. std::async provides safer exception handling and a direct return path via std::future, and where pausing and resuming is required, use coroutines. **(527, 531)**

- Explicitly specify std::launch::deferred or std::launch::async to force lazy or asynchronous evaluation of std::async calls. **(527)**

- Be aware of the braced alternative to object initialization. Instantiating a std::vector with predefined values is a good example of the convenience it can offer. **(529)**

Memory Management

- If you must create a pointer, prefer std::make_unique and std::make_shared to new. **(430, 513)**

- std::unique_ptr is a small, fast, move-only smart pointer for exclusive-ownership resource management. **(235)**

- std::shared_ptr is a slightly larger, reference-counted smart pointer for shared-ownership resource management. **(509)**

- Avoid C-style casting at all if you can, particularly with non-fundamental types. When casting classes, prefer static_cast (for derived-to-base upcasts), and dynamic_cast (for base-to-derived downcasts). **(517)**

- Where a raw pointer is unavoidable, stick it into a smart pointer as soon as possible. If that pointer cannot be deallocated with a standard delete call, add a custom deleter to the smart pointer.

PART TWO

LANGUAGE-AGNOSTIC BEST PRACTICES

CHAPTER FOUR

Project Development

Build a Solid Foundation

- Your project should build with a few, easy-to-perform steps.

Try to reduce the act of building your project down to a few, easy-to-perform steps, and consider adding a short "README" to the project describing the process to other developers.

- Add automatic code validation / static code analysis as part of your project's build.

Add to your project some form of automated code validation. This can either be a separate tool that you run against your project, or built into the compilation of your source code. Either way, try to incorporate running these checks as part of your project's build. This will allow you to fix each issue as soon as it is introduced, rather than letting them pile up and become unmanageable later.

• Build at the highest warning level tolerable.

Whether you're using compiler warnings or an external analyser, be sure to set the warning level of your chosen tool(s) as high as you can possibly tolerate, and prefer to resolve issues by fixing code rather than reducing the level.

• When it comes to using version control: commit everything, and commit often.

What you commit to your VCS should be anything (other than build artifacts of course) that undergoes change during the development of your software. That means: your project structure should not only comprise of code, it should incorporate its documentation as well, including any notes and to-do lists you feel are worth versioning.

This leaves you with an incredibly useful, combined history of all changes, for all elements of your product, and eliminates the redundancy of having to maintain each aspect of your project separately.

Committing changes often is a good habit to have for many more reasons, namely: it encourages a steady flow of updates into the project, resulting in small, easy-to-read diffs, it allows you and others to easily pick up from where you last left off, your latest work is always kept backed up safely on a secure remote server, and as long as you ensure that no commit breaks the build, it gives you the fine-grained ability to rollback changes one-by-one if needed.

Make All Interfaces User-Friendly

- Any good UI design begins with the design of a good API.

Whether or not your project has a UI, it almost certainly will have an API of some sort. While an API is the interface to your back-end, a UI is the interface to your API, hence, any good UI design begins with the design of a good API.

- When declaring functions: prefer simple over complex, be explicit rather than implicit, use standard types, and avoid long parameter lists.

A good interface should be easy to use correctly, and difficult to use incorrectly. To ensure this, prefer simple over complex, be explicit rather than implicit, use standard types in your function signatures as much as possible, and avoid long parameter lists.

- Every entity in your project should have only one well-defined, cohesive responsibility.

While every API is fundamentally made up of types and functions, depending on the programming language and paradigm used, they can be grouped or further broken down into a hierarchy of entities such as: frameworks, modules, libraries, namespaces, types / classes, prototypes, and structures.

Regardless of how your project is assembled, each entity should have only one well-defined, cohesive responsibility. Prefer creating small entities that closely model the problem domain, over large ones that are abstract in purpose. Small entities are easier to write, easier to test, and in the end, easier to use.

- Your API should exist to help its users, not to dump complex responsibilities onto them.

Try not to return results from functions that implicitly require careful management, such as: expecting users to destroy it in a particular manner, or trusting them not to change its state later. Possibly the worst offense you can commit in this respect, is giving out direct handles to your entities' internals, then expecting the receiver to behave with them.

- Only make public what should be public.

Only make public what should be public, and encapsulate the rest. You can hide an API's internals by placing them in files that are physically separate from its headers, or by using language features to logically restrict their visibility via the public interface. This gives you, as the developer, fine-grained access control over the private entities of your project, resulting in a safer, more reliable product for your users.

- Prefer dependency injection over inheritance, with the exception of abstract interfaces.

One way of avoiding strong coupling in your code, is to prefer dependency injection over inheritance where possible. A major exception to this rule of course is the abstract interface. Together with abstract interfaces, consider building an entity that provides a means for creating objects without having to specify their derived types (AKA an "Abstract Factory").

Put Your Interfaces to the Test

- Write tests in parallel with your code.

For every bug fix and feature you tackle, you should ensure at least two things: that the new code you add works correctly, and that by adding it, you do not break any existing code. This can be achieved by writing a set of tests that, when run, will execute a sequence of checks against your interfaces to verify the resulting behaviour is as expected.

Retrofitting tests to a project becomes increasingly difficult, sometimes even impossible, the longer it is put off. For that reason, writing tests should really form part of the development process itself. Of course, there are other reasons why tests should be written together with the features they probe: it forces you to see your user interface from the user's point of view, it gives developers a good feel of how the API is used, and while new tests verify that new functionality works, existing tests ensure that existing functionality is not broken by it.

- There are two main types of automated testing: unit and integration.

Unit testing verifies the behaviour of a software entity in isolation, while integration testing verifies the behaviour of multiple entities interacting with each other.

During unit testing, to ensure that an entity is properly isolated, its dependencies must be replaced by "mock" entities that exhibit well-defined test behaviour (This requirement is another circumstance where abstract interfaces and dependency injection become indispensable).

- When fixing a bug in your code, consider writing a regression test for it first.

When fixing a bug, a good first step is to write a "regression test" that exposes the issue. This test should simulate the conditions of the bug such that it is designed to fail. With this failing test in place, you can proceed with fixing the bug until it passes reliably.

- Don't be discouraged by how long it takes to develop tests.

It is perfectly acceptable for one to spend more time writing code that verifies logic, than it takes to implement the logic itself. As Albert Einstein put it: "If I had an hour to solve a problem, I'd spend 55 minutes thinking about the problem, and 5 minutes thinking about solutions".

- Error conditions should be tested as thoroughly as non-error conditions.

Tests should be written to enforce reliability. Reliable software not only means that it should work when expected to work, it also means failing safely when things go wrong. Well-defined error conditions are just as much a part of your product's intended functionality as its non-error conditions are, therefore, each should be tested as thoroughly as the other.

- Incorporate running tests as part of your project's build.

An automated test suite will allow you to ensure that, when making any changes to your code, the product remains in working order.

Also consider incorporating a good test coverage tool into your project's build. These tools are useful in pointing out which lines of code are not covered by your tests.

Implement to the Interface Design

- When defining functions: prefer simple over complex, safe over insecure, and correct over fast.

Write readable code. Legible code that is broken is still more valuable than illegible code that "just works".

For each feature you implement, prefer simple over complex, safe over insecure, and correct over fast. Avoid premature optimisation, as well as premature pessimization (Don't waste time guessing where pitfalls might be).

When writing functions: prefer short over long, and flat over nested. A complex function is a good indication that its entity does not have a single, cohesive responsibility, and therefore, should be broken down further into smaller parts.

- Establish a rational error handling policy for your project, and stick to it consistently.

Regardless of which policy you apply, errors should be emitted in a way that is as easy to catch, as they are easy to understand. Some details that are particularly useful in an error message are: a timestamp, an error type, its severity level, a detailed description of the error condition, and the position in code where the fault occurred (In fact, this sort of detail is useful in just about any log message your project emits).

It is also crucial that you do not penalise your users unnecessarily for low severity issues. Know when a function should rollback its changes and error out completely, and when it should simply emit a warning and continue.

- Strongly coupled code is difficult to maintain, and near impossible to reuse.

Forming relationships between the entities of a project is both natural and dangerous at the same time. Strongly coupled code is difficult to maintain, and near impossible to reuse. If any change made to one entity requires a significant understanding of any other entity, alarm bells should go off in your head.

- Avoid sharing global data between entities as much as possible.

Shared data not only increases coupling, it causes contention, which can needlessly reduce performance, but more importantly, can become extremely difficult to maintain.

Try to declare variables as locally to where they are needed as possible. The shorter their lifetimes, the less state you will have to maintain.

One exception to this rule is the use of globally shared constants. Contrary to what some people may believe, programming is not magic, so do try to avoid using magic numbers. Rather declare all required constants in some common area of your project where they are easy to find and adjust, than to have them scattered amongst your code as raw values.

- Don't sweat the small stuff.

When it comes to code formatting, naming conventions, and comment style, just pick a direction upfront, and keep consistent throughout the project. And for those engineers who arrive to the project later: When in Rome...

PART THREE

TEMPLATES & COMPILE-TIME PROGRAMMING

CHAPTER FIVE

Template Definitions

Why Use Templates?

Sometimes in software design we run into situations where one piece of code is required to act on or adapt to multiple types (E.g. generic algorithms and containers).

Templates are designed to solve this problem elegantly:

- Templates are functions (function templates), classes (class templates), or variables (variable templates) written *once* for use with multiple types.

- Because templates are language features, they are scope aware and type safe (unlike macros for example).

Templates also allow us to parameterize behavior as well as information, but more on this later.

Defining Function Templates

- A function template is a parameterized function that represents a family of functions rather than just one.

Consider a simple function that calculates the maximum between two values:

```
int Max( int a, int b )
{
  return a < b ? b : a;
}
```

This function however, restricts us to integers only. A more attractive solution would be one that could calculate the maximum between values of any type.

A simple function template to calculate the maximum between two values:

```
template <typename T>
T Max( T a, T b )
{
  return a < b ? b : a;
}
```

Of course, this function template will only work on values that are less-than comparable. One way to enforce this requirement is to specify a "concept" in the template signature:

```
template <typename T>
concept LessThanComparable = requires( T a, T b )
{
  { a < b } -> std::same_as<bool>;
};

template <typename T> requires LessThanComparable<T>
T Max( T a, T b )
{
  return a < b ? b : a;
}
```

Or perhaps, more simply, we could just restrict the parameter to arithmetic values:

```
template <typename T> requires std::is_arithmetic_v<T>
T Max( T a, T b )
{
  return a < b ? b : a;
}
```

- Concepts can be used to enforce requirements on one or more template parameters.

- Template parameters can be used within a function like any other type.

- Lambdas can be function templates too (known as "generic lambdas"):

```
auto Max = []<typename T>( T a, T b )
{
  return a < b ? b : a;
};
```

Using Function Templates

- When you pass function arguments, function templates are instantiated for those argument types implicitly.

- You can (and occasionally, need to) explicitly qualify template parameters.

Implicit qualification of template parameters from call arguments:

```
Max( 3, 7 ); // OK: T is int for both arguments
```

Explicit qualification of template parameters (when call arguments provide insufficient information):

```
Max( 3, 7.1 ); // ERROR: 1st T is int, 2nd T is double

Max<double>( 3, 7.1 ); // OK: T is double for both
```

A more flexible alternative may be to parameterize the return type and two separate input types:

```
template <typename R, typename T1, typename T2>
R Max( T1 a, T2 b )
{
  return a < b ? b : a;
}

//...

Max( 3, 7.1 ); // ERROR: no return type specified

Max<double>( 3, 7.1 ) // OK: return type is double
```

• A template is visited twice by the compiler. On first pass it's simply checked for correct syntax. It's only actually compiled when it is used (instantiated) in code.

Overloading Function Templates

- Like ordinary functions, you can overload function templates.

- When overloading function templates, limit your changes to the number of parameters…

```
template <typename T>
T Max( T a, T b, T c)
{
  return Max( Max( a, b ), c );
}
```

- …or to defining parameters explicitly:

```
double Max( double a, double b )
{
  return a < b ? b : a;
}
```

- Any call to a function template should match only one overload.

Declaring Class Templates

- A class template is a class with one or more type parameters left unspecified:

```cpp
template <typename T>
class Stack
{
public:

  // 1. defining a method inline

  void Push( const T& elem )
  {
    elements.push_back( elem );
  }

  void Pop();

private:
  std::vector<T> elements;
};

// 2. defining a method outside the class declaration

template <typename T>
void Stack<T>::Pop()
{
  elements.pop_back();
}
```

- Template parameters can be used within the class declaration like any other type.

Because a template can be used (thus compiled) from anywhere in code, the compiler needs access to its definition from anywhere. This is why template definitions are typically implemented in header files (more on this later).

Using Class Templates

- When using class templates, you pass the unspecified types as template arguments. The class template is then compiled (and instantiated) for those types:

```
Stack<int> intStack; // stack of ints

Stack<std::string> stringStack; // stack of strings

Stack<Stack<float>> floatStackStack; // stack o stacks
```

Note that each of these instantiations of Stack is a different type. You can't store them in a homogenous container for example. You could however, containerize them (as we'll soon see) using variadic templates.

- With class templates, only the methods that are called are actually instantiated (second pass compilation).

Consider a method on Stack that assigns a value in the container to zero:

```
template <typename T>
void Stack<T>::ZeroElement( int index )
{
  elements[ index ] = 0;
}
```

This method is invalid when the stack contains strings for example. However, if a Stack<std::string> is instantiated, and ZeroElement() is never called on that object, the code will still compile as the method will not be instantiated.

Specializing Class Templates

•   You can specialize class templates for certain types.

Booleans act weirdly in vectors, so you may want to use a deque instead when a bool template argument is provided:

```
template <>
class Stack<bool>
{

//...

private:
  std::deque<bool> elements;
};
```

- You can also partially specialize class templates for certain types:

```
// base declaration
template <typename T1, typename T2>
class Stack
{
  //...
};

// partial specialization: both types are the same
template <typename T>
class Stack<T, T>
{
  //...
};

// partial specialization: the 2nd type is int
template <typename T>
class Stack<T, int>
{
  //...
};

//...

Stack<int, float> a; // OK: matches <T1, T2>

Stack<float, float> b; // OK: matches <T, T>

Stack<float, int> c; // OK: matches <T, int>

Stack<int, int> d; // ERROR: matches <T, T> & <T, int>
```

- Any instantiation of a class template should match only one specialization.

NOTE: Function templates *cannot* be partially specialized, and even so, specialization is only applied to base function templates. On top of that, compilers prioritize overloading over specialization. So, the moral of the story is:

- Avoid specializing function templates, rather overload them.

Variable Templates

- A variable template is a parameterized variable that represents a family of variables rather than just one.

The most common use case for variable templates is parameterizing static consts. Take pi for example:

```
template <typename T>
static const T PI = T( 3.1415926535897932384626 );
```

We now have the ability to select a precision for pi at the point of instantiation:

```
auto intPi = PI<int>;
auto floatPi = PI<float>;
auto doublePi = PI<double>;
```

- Templates in general, can only be declared in global or namespace scope, and in class declarations. Variable templates in particular, must be declared static in the latter.

Template Code Organization

- As mentioned earlier, templates are typically implemented in header files so that the compiler can find their definitions from any point of instantiation. This is called "The Inclusion Model".

- "Explicit Instantiation" allows you to define template implementation in source files as long as you explicitly specify all types you wish to be instantiated:

```
// explicitly instantiate Max() for int

template int Max( int, int );

// explicitly instantiate ALL methods of Stack

template class Stack<float>;
```

```
// explicitly instantiate certain methods of Stack

template Stack<std::string>::Stack();

template void Stack<std::string>::Push( const
std::string& );
```

CHAPTER SIX

Template Parameters

Default Template Arguments

- You can define default arguments for template parameters. These may even refer to previous template parameters:

```cpp
template <typename T, typename C = std::vector<T>>
class Stack
{

//...

private:
  C elements;
};

//...

Stack<float, std::deque<float>> floatDeque;
Stack<float> floatVector; // C = std::vector<float>
```

Template Template Parameters

• A template parameter can also be a template itself.

The second specification of "float" here is redundant as we already know the contained type from the first argument:

```
Stack<float, std::deque<float>> floatDeque;
```

To remove this redundancy, we can use a template template parameter:

```
template <typename T, template <typename Elem>
typename C = std::vector>
class Stack
{

//...

private:
  C<T> elements;
};

//...

Stack<float, std::deque> floatDeque;
```

Nontype Template Parameters

- Templates can also have parameters that are values rather than types:

```
template <typename T, int Size>
class Stack
{

//...

private:
  T elements[ Size ];
};
```

- Like regular template parameters, you can define default arguments for nontype parameters as well:

```
template <typename T, int Size = 100>
class Stack
{
  //...
}

//...

Stack<double, 256> doubleStack;

Stack<float> floatStack; // 100 used as 2nd argument
```

- You can even use auto as a nontype template parameter:

```
template <auto Msg>
void Print()
{
  std::cout << Msg << std::endl;
}

//...

Print<3>(); // auto -> int
Print<'2'>(); // auto -> char
Print<true>(); // auto -> bool
```

Template Parameter Packs (Variadic Templates)

- A template parameter pack (donated by "...") can represent any number of parameters of any type.

- Templates that use parameter packs are called "variadic templates".

Earlier I mentioned that one use case for variadic templates could be to containerize objects of different type. Let's have a look at how this may be done:

```
template <typename... T>
class GenericContainer
{
public:
  GenericContainer( const T&... elems )
  {
    elements.insert( elements.end(), { elems... } );
  }
  GenericContainer() = default;

private:
  std::vector<std::variant<T...>> elements;
};
```

We can then instantiate (and populate) the container via our user-defined constructor like so (implicit qualification of template parameters from constructor arguments):

```
GenericContainer stacks( intStack, stringStack,
floatStackStack );
```

While this is nice, it won't allow for multiple arguments of the same type as our "elements" variant requires that all parameters be unique. Thus, again, occasionally explicit qualification of template parameters is necessary:

```
GenericContainer<Stack<int>, Stack<std::string>,
Stack<Stack<float>>> stacks;
```

Now let's add a separate method to populate the container:

```
template <typename... T>
class GenericContainer
{
public:
//...

  template <typename... Elem>
  void Push( const Elem&... elems )
  {
    elements.insert( elements.end(), { elems... } );
  }

//...
};
//...

stacks.Push( intStack, intStack, stringStack,
floatStackStack ); // OK: multiple intStacks allowed
```

Suppose we wanted to add a convenience method that populates the container with one of each element type. One way to do this could be to simply forward the class template parameter pack to our Push() method:

```
template <typename... T>
class GenericContainer
{
public:
//...

  void PushOneOfEach()
  {
    Push( T()... );
  }

//...
};
```

Another could be to iterate through the parameter pack using recursion:

```cpp
template <typename... T>
class GenericContainer
{
public:

//...

  void PushOneOfEach()
  {
    PushRecursive<T...>();
  }

//...

private:

  template <typename E1, typename E2, typename... Es>
  void PushRecursive()
  {
    PushRecursive<E1>();
    PushRecursive<E2, Es...>();
  }

  template <typename Elem>
  void PushRecursive()
  {
    Push( Elem() );
  }

//...

};
```

- To process variadic template parameters, you need to use recursion and / or a matching non-variadic function / method.

CHAPTER SEVEN

Beyond Templates

Compile-Time Programming

- As we've seen, templates can give us the ability to execute logical operations such as conditionals, selections, and iterations at compile-time.

- Tools such as constexpr and consteval provide even further support for compile-time computing.

A great example of the power constexpr gives us (over any wacky equivalent "template metaprogramming"), is the ability to execute ordinary-looking code at compile-time:

```
constexpr bool IsPrimeNumber( int x )
{
  for ( int d = 2; d <= x / 2; d++ )
  {
    if ( x % d == 0 )
    {
      return false;
    }
  }
  return x > 1;
}

//...

bool isFivePrime = IsPrimeNumber( 5 );
```

Note however, that the value of IsPrimeNumber() is not guaranteed to be evaluated at compile-time. To ensure compile-time evaluation, we can either specify our assignment as a constexpr itself...

```
constexpr bool isFivePrime = IsPrimeNumber( 5 );
```

...or define IsPrimeNumber() as consteval:

```
consteval bool IsPrimeNumber( int x )
{
  //...
}
```

- A constexpr function (or lambda for that matter) may be either compile-time or runtime invoked.

- A consteval function (or "immediate function") can only be compile-time invoked, *and* must return a constant.

Compile-Time Debugging

C++ compile-time programming is essentially the process of using the compiler as an interpreter. As with any interpreter, when the compiler executes logic that is malformed, it returns a backtrace of the issue (here, in the form of a compilation error).

It won't take you long to run into some very large and unwieldy backtraces when compile-time programming. Unfortunately (at least for now) this is just the way it is. I have found however, that some compilers can do a better job of describing certain issues than others. My advice is:

- Have more than one compiler handy when compile-time programming. When you hit a build issue you can't understand, try another compiler.

Summary

Modern C++ Coding Standards

- Use #pragma once at the top of every header to ensure that the file is included only once per compilation.
- #include as little as possible in your headers. Prefer to forward declare. This not only improves compilation time, but honours the greater rule of: "only make public what should be public".
- Avoid global using's in a header (That goes for namespaces and for aliases). They will pollute the global namespace of all source files that include it.
- Avoid declaring methods virtual until you have a valid and compelling reason for it. An abstract base class is a good example of such.

- Explicitly declare overriding functions override. It's often better to be explicit than implicit.
- Child classes should inherit to be re-usable, not to re-use. If a class is not designed to be a parent, use final to block any further inheritance.
- Don't use private or protected inheritance. Keep it simple, always public inherit, and use multiple inheritance judiciously.
- Compilers implicitly generate a default constructor, destructor, copy constructor, and copy operator. Rather be explicit with them upfront, than face any nasty surprises later.
- Compilers will only implicitly generate a default move constructor and operator if there are no explicit destructors, copy constructors, or copy operators. However, if a class contains any non-movable, non-static members, the move operator will be deleted.
- Always make base class destructors public and virtual. This avoids memory leaking when an instance of a derived class is deleted through a pointer to its base.
- Class copying is tricky. As a rule-of-thumb, disable copy operators upfront with =delete, and re-enable

them only if your class absolutely requires it later.

- Consider using the explicit keyword before the declaration of any constructor with a single argument. This avoids classes being constructed implicitly by value.

- Never throw an exception from the destructor, and never call a virtual method from either the constructor or the destructor.

- All classes, whether public or private, should belong to a namespace. Explicitly draw project boundary lines.

- Always declare class members private. Again: "only make public what should be public".

- Use the "pImpl" idiom to keep implementation details (private methods and members) out of public headers.

- Try to avoid using friend classes. They tend to indicate poor design, and can allow users to gain access to all protected and private members of your API.

- Prefer enum class over enum. They're type safe, and can be forward-declared unlike regular enums.

- Prefer enums to booleans in method signatures to improve code readability, usability and safety.

- Ensure that your API is const correct. That goes for both method const-ness as well as parameter const-ness.

- Prefer passing a non-trivial, non-mutable object as a const reference over passing it by value. This avoids the unnecessary overhead of copying the object into the method.

- Avoid using inline methods until you have proven that your code has a significant performance issue, and have confirmed that inlining fixes it.

- To guarantee completeness of your own headers, the order of items at the top of a source file should go: Your header #includes, third-party header #includes, standard header #includes, usings, then static consts.

- Always prefer to #include using angle brackets over quotation marks. Project include paths should be configured in project config.

- Don't pull in third-party dependencies unnecessarily. If there's already a standard feature available for what you need, use it.

- Use static consts instead of #define macros. A #define is just dumb text-replacement, it does not define an actual object.

- All methods and members of a private pImpl class can be declared public as they are already only accessible to the owning class.
- In-class initialize where possible. It is generally a good idea to initialize a variable on the same line that it is declared.
- Where in-class initialization is not possible, prefer constructor initialization to assignment. This avoids unnecessary run-time overhead.
- Always define methods in a .cpp file, even if they are just =default. This will keep the option of making changes to them open, without having to break the public interface.
- Prefer lock guards and / or std::atomic variables over manual mutex locking and unlocking.
- The container rule-of-thumb: When in doubt use std::vector. Otherwise, choose a content-appropriate alternative (such as std::map or std::string).
- Adopt a const iterator model for traversing linear data structures. Range-for loops have simpler syntax, and are generally faster and safer than indexed for loops.
- Prefer aliases over typedefs, and again, do not

use #define macros. Alias syntax is simpler than typedef, especially with templated types.

- auto and decltype are great tools to have, but like templates, be aware of how they infer their types - e.g. decltype(auto) retains references and cv-qualifiers, while auto does not.

- In 99% of cases auto just works, but sometimes it makes more sense to be explicit.

- Use std::function in place of old-style function pointers, and prefer lambdas over std::bind where anonymous functions are required.

- Prefer nullptr to NULL. The former is an actual null object, the latter is nothing more than a #define for the literal 0.

- Prefer task-based programming to thread-based where possible. std::async provides safer exception handling and a direct return path via std::future, and where pausing and resuming is required, use coroutines.

- Explicitly specify std::launch::deferred or std::launch::async to force lazy or asynchronous evaluation of std::async calls.

- Be aware of the braced alternative to object initialization. Instantiating a std::vector with predefined values is a good example of the convenience it can offer.

- If you must create a pointer, prefer std::make_unique and std::make_shared to new.

- std::unique_ptr is a small, fast, move-only smart pointer for exclusive-ownership resource management.

- std::shared_ptr is a slightly larger, reference-counted smart pointer for shared-ownership resource management.

- Avoid C-style casting at all if you can, particularly with non-fundamental types. When casting classes, prefer static_cast (for derived-to-base upcasts), and dynamic_cast (for base-to-derived downcasts).

- Where a raw pointer is unavoidable, stick it into a smart pointer as soon as possible. If that pointer cannot be deallocated with a standard delete call, add a custom deleter to the smart pointer.

Language-Agnostic Best Practices

- Your project should build with a few, easy-to-perform steps.
- Add automatic code validation / static code analysis as part of your project's build.
- Build at the highest warning level tolerable.
- When it comes to using version control: commit everything, and commit often.
- Any good UI design begins with the design of a good API.
- When declaring functions: prefer simple over complex, be explicit rather than implicit, use standard types, and avoid long parameter lists.
- Every entity in your project should have only one well-defined, cohesive responsibility.
- Your API should exist to help its users, not to dump complex responsibilities onto them.
- Only make public what should be public.
- Prefer dependency injection over inheritance, with the exception of abstract interfaces.
- Write tests in parallel with your code.
- There are two main types of automated testing: unit and integration.

- When fixing a bug in your code, consider writing a regression test for it first.
- Don't be discouraged by how long it takes to develop tests.
- Error conditions should be tested as thoroughly as non-error conditions.
- Incorporate running tests as part of your project's build.
- When defining functions: prefer simple over complex, safe over insecure, and correct over fast.
- Establish a rational error handling policy for your project, and stick to it consistently.
- Strongly coupled code is difficult to maintain, and near impossible to reuse.
- Avoid sharing global data between entities as much as possible.
- Don't sweat the small stuff.

Templates & Compile-Time Programming

- Templates are functions (function templates), classes (class templates), or variables (variable templates) written *once* for use with multiple types.
- Because templates are language features, they are scope aware and type safe (unlike macros for example).
- A function template is a parameterized function that represents a family of functions rather than just one.
- Concepts can be used to enforce requirements on one or more template parameters.
- Template parameters can be used within a function like any other type.
- Lambdas can be function templates too (known as "generic lambdas").
- When you pass function arguments, function templates are instantiated for those argument types implicitly.
- You can (and occasionally, need to) explicitly qualify template parameters.
- A template is visited twice by the compiler. On first pass it's simply checked for correct syntax. It's only

actually compiled when it is used (instantiated) in code.

- Like ordinary functions, you can overload function templates.

- When overloading function templates, limit your changes to the number of parameters or to defining parameters explicitly.

- Any call to a function template should match only one overload.

- A class template is a class with one or more type parameters left unspecified.

- Template parameters can be used within the class declaration like any other type.

- When using class templates, you pass the unspecified types as template arguments. The class template is then compiled (and instantiated) for those types.

- With class templates, only the methods that are called are actually instantiated (second pass compilation).

- You can specialize class templates for certain types.

- You can also partially specialize class templates for certain types.

- Any instantiation of a class template should match

only one specialization.

- Avoid specializing function templates, rather overload them.

- A variable template is a parameterized variable that represents a family of variables rather than just one.

- Templates in general, can only be declared in global or namespace scope, and in class declarations. Variable templates in particular, must be declared static in the latter.

- As mentioned earlier, templates are typically implemented in header files so that the compiler can find their definitions from any point of instantiation. This is called "The Inclusion Model".

- "Explicit Instantiation" allows you to define template implementation in source files as long as you explicitly specify all types you wish to be instantiated.

- You can define default arguments for template parameters. These may even refer to previous template parameters.

- A template parameter can also be a template itself.

- Templates can also have parameters that are values rather than types.

- Like regular template parameters, you can define default arguments for nontype parameters as well.
- You can even use auto as a nontype template parameter.
- A template parameter pack (donated by "...") can represent any number of parameters of any type.
- Templates that use parameter packs are called "variadic templates".
- To process variadic template parameters, you need to use recursion and / or a matching non-variadic function / method.
- As we've seen, templates can give us the ability to execute logical operations such as conditionals, selections, and iterations at compile-time.
- Tools such as constexpr and consteval provide even further support for compile-time computing.
- A constexpr function (or lambda for that matter) may be either compile-time or runtime invoked.
- A consteval function (or "immediate function") can only be compile-time invoked, *and* must return a constant.
- Have more than one compiler handy when compile-time programming. When you hit a build issue you can't understand, try another compiler.